Hijacked

How A Contractor Was Hijacked and Robbed Blind By His Own Business

Arne Raisanen

How a contractor was hijacked and robbed blind by his own business

HIJACKED

Business

By Arne Raisanen

Publisher: Arne Raisanen

Book design: Arne Raisanen

ISBN: 978-0-9914289-1-5

First edition

Short story

Printed in the United States of America

How a contractor was hijacked and robbed blind by his own business

How a contractor

was hijacked

and

robbed blind

by his own business.

How a contractor was hijacked and robbed blind by his own business

Keep your thinking right and your business will be right.

Zig Ziglar

A J just didn't get it; his business started out debt free. For years he never borrowed a dime. It felt like the more he grew, the more debt he took on. AJ couldn't figure out why? He was closing plenty of sales and was definitely not the cheapest guy around.

Now he was in a dilemma and he had no solutions.

He did not realize it yet, but he was handcuffed and hijacked by his own business.

His story began like many small businesses....

Become the kind of leader that people would follow voluntarily, even if you had no title or position

Brian Tracey

AJ was a technician by trade and a salesman at heart! He truly enjoyed solving problems with real solutions for his clients. With his technical background he could figure just about anything out. Even at a young age AJ's mind worked like a businessman.

The entrepreneurial spirit in him was running high!

As a young boy selling newspapers, he enjoyed the action of collecting the money for each paper sold.

Fast forward a few years: AJ discovered he thoroughly enjoyed in-home service selling.

He worked his way into the heating and plumbing industry: first on installation projects, earning his masters license, and eventually finding in-home sales and service repairs to be his passion. Often times clients had problems that other competitors didn't seem to care about or want to fix. Soon AJ became known as the guy who would take the time to find the solution rather than put a Band-Aid on it. It wasn't long before clients would call for service and ask for AJ specifically.

AJ never really thought about owning his own business at the time, but clients were telling him he should. He was the one doing the work anyway! A short time later, circumstances as well as timing, put AJ in a place where his options to start his own business were looking him straight in the eyes.

Henry Ford once said,

"If you think you can do a thing, or you can't do a thing,

you're right.' "

A new business was born!

AJ heating & plumbing business started out of his home. Because he was moving along in his new venture and had hardly a clue what to do, it started out a little rocky.. he had very little capital to begin with, just an old pickup truck plus a few tools. His plan was as empty as a white sheet of paper without much business

knowledge to lean on… but slowly the business grew.

He spent the first few months trying to drum up some business, talking with anyone who would listen. Clients who hired him would tell their neighbors about his services. Slowly the word got around that there was a new business in town.

AJ wasn't even sure where his prices should be or what he should charge for service. So he did what most new business owners would do. He found out what his competitors were charging and based his prices around theirs. His thought was this; they must know what to charge – they are in business, right?

His motto in his business was simple; AJ wanted to treat others like he would want to be treated.

It didn't take long before his client base started to grow; word of mouth was by far his best marketing! He would do a service call for one client, and before long their neighbors would be calling for some type of service. His name became the "GUY WHO COULD FIX IT"; It amazed him how his client base was growing.

AJ realized he was going to need more help in-order to take care of his clients... Again new territory along with uncertainty on what to do. He was busy; the phone was ringing off the hook! He was also aware that if he hired someone, he would have to purchase another vehicle along with more tools.

AJ hired his first employee. The phone rang and rang - more work, more work, piles of work…. AJ hired his second employee, service calls still rang…. Then third employee, fourth….

KEY POINT:

Having a clear vision with a working budget, is extremely important to grow a successful business.

More vehicles, more tools, more hiring!

The first year his sales were not even a $100K. It wasn't long before his annual sales were over a million dollars.

As the business grew AJ needed to think about hiring managers along with office staff to take care of the day to day duties. This wasn't something that had crossed his mind! He also needed office space to do this. He was running out of room! AJ built a new building which included extra warehouse space and offices. He then hired a service manager, and a receptionist – another foreign territory to encounter.

AJ was excited with the new professional appearance of his business along with his clients!

Within a short period of time clients started stopping in to purchase "do it yourself" plumbing parts from AJ's.

AJ could see another business opportunity. Why not open a retail store? He could take care of "do it yourself" walk-in clients, plus he would have better purchasing power with his vendors.

He understood the volume game - the more you buy the less you pay!

Purchasing a franchise hardware chain, his retail business was born! His thinking went this way: he already had people in the office so why not cover their wages through the retail side of the business? The office people could cover the phones as well as take care of walk in retail clients. It made sense to him, plus he could have better purchasing power, often times bypassing the middle guy - going straight to the manufacturer for a more competitive price.

It happened many times, a retail client would end up becoming a service client, confirming what AJ figured would happen by opening his retail store business.

A few years later an opportunity came up to buy an existing retail store. This store had a small service business with it. AJ talked with his banker and they decided it was an opportunity too good to pass up!

The first year sales growth was unbelievable - which was fascinating to AJ.

His stores were packed with product - from nuts and bolts to washers, dryers, plumbing, heating, electrical, paint, tools, and everything you would find in a hardware store.

Sales grew to over 2 million the next year, business was booming! The phone was always ringing for service or sales.

As AJ's business grew so did the debt, yet his banker continued to lend him money every time the business would grow. His banker would always say, "you can cash flow it, so go ahead."

AJ relied on the advice of his banker, considering he himself had very little knowledge of business. Every step he took in his business was new territory with many learning curves and bumps as he went. AJ needed someone to help him with his business decisions. He realized later, much later that a bank is in the business of lending money! That is how they make their money by lending to guys like AJ and earning interest on the borrowed money.

The First Red Flags in AJ's Business:

AJ began to notice something – every now and again he would have these cash-flow problems when the bills were due. There wasn't sufficient money to pay them! Either it was on accounts receivable or tied up in inventory. Talking with his banker he was told he needed a line of credit to solve his cash-flow issues. After he opened a line of credit with the bank, His problem was solved for a while. Not long after that a pattern began to form. When ever he would use his line of credit.

It seemed AJ could never pay it all back in the same month, sometimes only paying the interest! Cash just seemed to go through the check book like water in a leaky bucket, never staying in the check book. Every few months AJ was using his line of credit to make payroll and pay the bills. It became harder and harder to pay down the line of credit. Eventually all he could pay was interest, which was amounting to quite a bit of money every month.

The Second Red Flag in AJ's Business:

A few months later he received a call from his banker. The banks board didn't like the risk he was to them! His banker explained that AJ was not using the line of credit correctly. He continued by saying that the board was thinking about calling in his loans! AJ couldn't believe this was happening.

He had an emergency meeting with his banker, who agreed to extend his loans, at a much higher interest rate.

Both AJ and his banker felt things would improve in AJ,s business over the next few months, once the cash flow increased. He did have a lot on accounts owed to him, plus sales were still increasing!

Cash flow was still a mystery to AJ - he just believed his banker; but really didn't understand how any of this worked.

14

Even though AJ didn't understand cash flow, he needed money. He didn't really have a choice either way! He owed the bank a lot of money, plus he had to find a quick fix to keep going.

AJ was an optimist. He figured once the cash came in he would pay back the line of credit; it would get better - yes it would get better! He would get this figured out - just give him time.

The reality - things didn't get better - they actually got worse! Pretty soon vendors were calling because AJ couldn't pay them on time. Every other month he would be put on credit hold with vendors until he paid them some money.

The crazy part; his business was known for doing great service, reputable work. It wasn't like the money wasn't coming in, no his sales were growing, but somehow it just disap-peared!

He was being robbed, he didn't even know how or who it was until later, much later.

He found out that some thug by the name of **Interest,** had a friend called **Overhead** and together they had AJ handcuffed and were hijacking his business.

His business was like a bottomless pit! Every dollar that came into his business was being robbed by Interest and Overhead.

Oh, they did have a few other friends also, another cigar-smoking fat cat called Debt was taking his fair share. A skinny street urchin called Fees, seemed to pop up every time Debt came around if he couldn't get his money.

For some reason Debt had a set amount he took every month! And, to top that, there was a legal thief by the name of Payroll Tax. This guy was brutal – the more employees AJ had the more this guy took! Besides, if you were a day late he would send his boss named IRS after you!

AJ had many sleepless nights, He almost had a nervous breakdown, He suffered two mini strokes. It seemed like it was one thing after another with his health.

He felt like the whole world was on his back, he couldn't move. He wasn't sure what to do.

He kept looking at his business and wondering where he could cut expenses. What was the quick fix, or was there one?

These criminals that were in his business - Debt & Interest were relentless and ruthless, plus cash flow was not getting better.

AJ was not the only one who was worried….

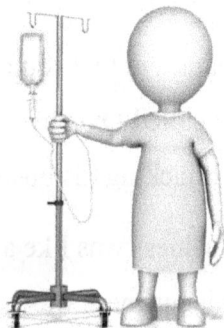

16

It had been months since AJ had taken a regular paycheck.

His poor wife was stressing over how they would make the next mortgage payment? How would they feed the children?

Cash was becoming scarce around AJ's business, every dollar that came in went to pay bills! There was never enough to pay all the bills.

Something had to change!

AJ was still an optimist; thinking things were going to get better, although he wasn't sure how!

AJ knew he needed help in his business. Someone whose knowledge was greater than his.

Something had to change!

AJ also realized he needed an expert who could go though his business, find out why his cash flow was non-existent, and figure out how to pay all this debt back. Plus he knew his health wasn't getting any better either.

AJ talked with a mentor whom he had full confidence in, asking him what he thought he should do? His mentor advised him to hire someone to go through his whole business, as well as putting a plan together. He needed business help!

The Day of a new beginning:

After doing research AJ hired a company who came highly recommended.

Picking up the phone he dialed the number of the recommended company. When the line was answered, AJ stated his business needs help. AJ started to feel a little better!

The next day:

AJ sat in his office looking across his desk at a coach who had been sent to help him in his business. This guy was pleasant, but all business. He was also smart!

He knew almost instantly there were guys in AJ's business who had AJ in handcuffs, and were literally robbing him blind.

This Coach was brilliant, he even knew their names!

There was Debt, Interest, Liability, along with a few others he mentioned.

This Coach figured out who these culprits were in the blink of an eye. How in the world did this guy know so fast how these culprits were responsible for his problems? AJ wondered...

And, how was he going to get rid of them? What would AJ have to do? He was a little bit nervous to say the least! All this confusion made his head spin.

Coach went on about some hero AJ needed to know who could stop these guys from stealing him blind. Some knew this hero as Business Management. He would teach AJ how to collar these criminals along with stopping the cash from disappearing.

AJ pondered the thought. He did have to do something! He was extremely excited as well as apprehensive. He knew he wanted help, but wasn't sure how he himself was going to have to change.

Coach was pretty clever when finding these bad guys, and he did promise he could help AJ, but first he had a serious question for him.

Coach: "AJ! - Are you willing to change the way you're running your business?"

AJ: "Yes"

Coach: "Are you sure?"

AJ: "Yes, Yes I am!"

Coach: "AJ you don't have a problem with money coming in your business. Your biggest issue is you have more money going out than coming in! You need to stop the bleeding (output) in order to get a handle on your business."

"AJ was pondering these last few words." He needed to stop the bleeding to get a handle on his business. So in other words, he had money coming in but his debt was eating up all the money! It made sense...

19

"AJ here is what I'm going to do, I'm going to bring our hero, Business Management, tomorrow." coach explained. "This guy is the answer to your problems. He will have a couple of other hero's with him named Budget and Vision. Together with your help, they will identify where these robbers hide out, along with giving you the tools to get rid of them!

We have another hero named Strong Sales, but he isn't needed, you have proven you know how to sell!"

AJ was all ears, but a little hesitant, because he knew these guys were going to be expensive.

"How much money would this cost me, and how in the world will I afford it?" stressed AJ.

"Here is how it works; any investment you make with us, has a guarantee of a two to one return in the first year". Proclaimed coach.

It was risk free. AJ had nothing to lose.

Sure enough the next-day AJ's new coach John showed up with a helper Trig; she was to help compile all the things that Coach John needed to help AJ fix his problems.

Coach John meant business, working AJ like a dog, long days, plenty of homework with non-stop training.

The first snap shot reports were not only eye opening but gut wrenching to say the least. The picture was ugly!

Coach John showed AJ how the Debt along with Interest had increased the liability of his company, pointing out that the net worth was literally nothing!

AJ vaguely remembers his banker saying something about net worth, but didn't really understand at the time what net worth was, or how it could affect his cash-flow problem.

Coach John compiled all kinds of numbers and charts, explaining to AJ how the criminals snuck their way into his business.

He also showed AJ how overhead really worked. It was in AJ's hands to control the overhead or if he wanted to be competitive as well as profitable in his market place.

Coach John describes that as a business grows, overhead loves to grow also.

"How do we get rid of it?" questions AJ.

"While we can't just get rid of it, we can however control it so it doesn't just run wild; just like we can control your payroll taxes, insurance, wages." "In fact", John points out "if you could control the Liability in your company, you can control overhead pretty easily."

Trig stayed silent the whole time while she was gathering everything that Coach John needed.

Finally piping up, Trig challenged AJ about his vision. She was asking questions about his goals, projections, time tables... all a language he had a hard time understanding.

AJ wondered, "what did this have to do with his problems right now?"

However AJ assumed it must be important since Coach John was agreeing with Trig.

Coach John was awesome – the more AJ learned from him, the more he was convinced. John had all the answers to solving AJ's problems.

He also knew that Trig had something he needed to learn too, but she would have to do some more explaining before AJ understood the importance of what she was saying.

Coach John did give AJ some credit! He strongly believed that AJ's greatest attribute was his selling skills. He felt this was more than likely what kept the business going for so long! AJ was pretty good at closing sales. It was not because he was the low-price guy. No, AJ knew how to sell for a profit!

John brings out, "Although sales are a very important part of business, there are other factors that need to be in place in order for a business to survive."

Trig piped up, "AJ - if you want to succeed in business, you first need to know where you're going. You also need to know how you're going to get there, as well as what it will look like when you get there!"

> **KEY POINT:**
>
> Your business plan needs to be crystal clear as to where you're going, how are you going to get there, and what will it look like when you get there.

Coach John claims: if AJ follows the plan they set forth, he would have a two to one return on his investment with-in the next 12 months!

...Fast forward twelve months...

AJ had a TEN to ONE return on his investment with Coach John!

You see, AJ had very little business experience. He also did not understand how overhead or debt would affect the cost of running a business.

His skills involved sales along with his technical knowledge, where AJ excelled. Even Coach John could see that! Coach John had watched AJ do a complete sales presentation, telling him later that AJ could teach others how to sell!

KEY POINT:

Having a crystal clear understanding of your overhead in your business is vital to your success!

AJ also learned a lot about budgets and business visions, along with business planning.

One eye-opening moment that really stood out to AJ, was when Coach John announced "A business that grows too fast can easily get out of control."

AJ's business was living proof: His sales had increased over 70% in one year! John explained that when a business grows too fast, overhead becomes "the King". John explained "the King" will take the cash away from all the other parts of the business that need cash to function!

Coach John also explained to AJ: Cash Flow has no back-bone. Who ever could win him over, got the cash! He added, "The only way to make sure cash flow was on your side was to take Trigs advice. Put it all down on paper, show the Cash where it needs to go before you actually spend it."

KEY POINT:

Controlling your business growth will keep you in control of your business. If you're not in control, overhead can overtake your business and spin it out of control

John also warned, if you don't control your cash flow, the debt along with interest will get out of control again.

He also put a business plan together for AJ and showed him how it worked. John explained in order for AJ to grow his business profitably, he needed a business plan. A plan that was crystal clear yet measurable, which went along with AJ's dreams he had for his business.

AJ admitted he never really had a plan, he was just flying by the seat of his pants! Trig chuckled, "You are no different than 80% of all small business who are having cash flow issues."

Coach John also demonstrated to AJ how he was going to change his business over the next few years, how his budgeting together with his management systems would continue to help AJ get over his cash flow issues. He also clarified that if AJ used the budget as a working tool, it would be a lot easier to manage as he moved forward in his business. One important factor Coach John expressed about budgeting: it had to be a live budget, not something you put together and forget about.

Goals

1. Sales System
2. Running Budget
3. Business Vision

Coach John informed, sometimes debt is not such a bad guy and even interest can be ok once in awhile, but if AJ really followed his advice, he probably would never have to get too friendly with debt or interest again.

Coach John implied, even with all AJ had learned, his business was still pretty fragile; therefore it wouldn't take much to put AJ back into a cash flow issue again.

Coach John stopped the bleeding in AJ's company, he cut overhead where it was heavy. He streamlined his business with measurable gauges for AJ to use.

He cautioned AJ, explaining that his debt load was dangerously high. As long as the sales revenues were sustained in his company, the chances were pretty high that AJ would recover from his bad debt issues.

AJ's one-year checkup rated a A+! Everything was on track, as well as the debt was going down.

> **KEY POINT:**
>
> Measuring and tracking is critical to obtain accurate results in your business.

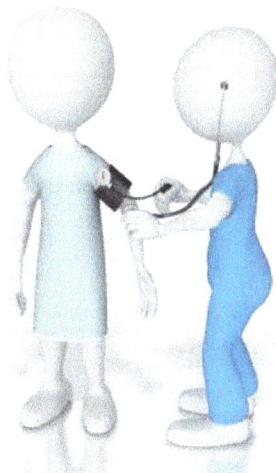

AJ felt the pressure decrease. Things were still tight, but he no longer was having the cash flow issues like before. He knew where every dollar that came into his business was going before he ever wrote a check.

He had systems for each department in his business. Each month he would sit down with P/L (Profit & Loss) statements for each department. AJ Entered this information into his master bottom up budget calculator. He could see how each part of his business was working. If one department didn't make the budget that month, he would adjust the numbers for the next month to stay in the black. (*positive*)

In the next three years, AJ had paid off over 50% of the debt. He was on schedule to be out of the bad debt in three more years. His Banker was ecstatic with his new management skills.

AJ was still worried about the debt, he knew that if any big shake up in the economy came, he would once again be in trouble.

With the training AJ received, along with the tools, he now had a very keen knowledge of where he was in his business at all times. He knew what numbers to be watching in his balance sheets. No more guessing or wondering.

Another formerly unknown aspect AJ discovered was the ability to understand what his labor burden was in each of his departments. This really helped when he needed to make price adjustments.

It would be nice to end this story on a happy note saying AJ's business survived. If this were the case, AJ would've been the first one to give all the credit to Coach John and Trig, but things didn't turn out that way.

In fact, not too many businesses have seen a worse economy coming since the thirties.

AJ's didn't make it.

The businesses that did survive had very manageable debt or no debt at all. AJ's debt however was bad, so when the economy started to fall, there simply wasn't a banker willing to risk spreading his debt over a longer period.

Even his banker, who had seen AJ's business transformation was unwilling to loan him money! Oh No! The banks were pulling in the reins, and anyone who was remotely high risk they didn't want to touch. They had their ratios as to who they would lend money or extend credit.

AJ was high risk to the bank.

The End of AJ's Business:

AJ's main clientele were higher-end clients "who had vacation lake homes" with their main homes in the city. When the economy started to falter, his high end clients started cutting back.

They were cutting their expenses also. Some lost their lake homes back to the banks. Many just stopped doing remodels or additions to their lake homes. Others cut maintenance programs to save money.

This was all a big part of AJ's business.

The next year AJ's sales dropped by over 50%!

People who had money were stuffing it under their mattress waiting to see what was going to happen.

Those who had too much debt went broke!

AJ clearly remembers what Coach John said; "If something happened in the economy, he might be in trouble."

AJ was in enormous trouble!

The big difference now was AJ knew what was happening in his business. He fully understood cash flow!

He called an emergency meeting with his banker to find out what they wanted him to do! He explained to his banker he only had a few weeks left of cash flow, if something didn't change he would go broke.

The final meeting:

AJ's banker along with the banker's finance person looked over his financial statements, not saying much at all.

AJ could see they were a little confused.

After what felt like forever the banker said; "You're not behind on your loans with us!"

AJ objected, "Right now I am not, but next month there will be no cash to pay you unless something changes."

The clock….. ticked in silence for quite awhile, nobody was saying anything. AJ's banker finally spoke; "Can I make a suggestion?"

AJ replied, "of course", wondering what his banker was going to say.

His banker stated, "AJ - I would like to make a suggestion that you hire an attorney."

AJ was a little confused with the banker's suggestion, finding out later that his banker was telling him to file bankruptcy!

Bankruptcy was not what AJ was thinking! Here he had paid off over 50% of the debt, surely the bank would work with him.

But he was wrong!

The low point in AJ's life:

AJ found an attorney who had glanced over his business books. He put his glasses down. Looking at AJ and his wife he explained, "Your banker is looking out for you! Your banker has seen how your business turned around. He personally witnessed how your debt was being paid down. He also knows it wasn't possible to sustain the debt payoff with your sales dropping by 50%".

On top of everything the economy was sinking really fast.

The attorney explained how AJ would have to file personal bankruptcy.

One week after AJ and his wife signed the bankruptcy paperwork, AJ's banker came over to visit. He asked AJ if he had filed, and AJ replied "yes".

"AJ you have a wife and a family to take care of" He commented with concern.

He went on saying, if AJ ever wanted to start another business the bank was willing to help him.

AJ was stunned at his banker's vote of confidence, he thanked him before leaving to pick up the pieces and put his life back together. He really did have to put his life back together! It was a low point in AJ's life, he knew the road before him would have speed bumps and pot holes.

Obstacles are the things we see when we take our eyes off our goals.
Zig Ziglar

It could have ended worse!

AJ was truly hijacked and robbed blind by his own business.

He ended up losing almost everything, losing his house, his truck, the family vehicle! However he did have his children - along with his wonderful wife who was a very understanding friend.

AJ did start over. Looking back he can definitely see the value in all the teachings he not only received from John & Trig, but the real life experiences he will never forget.

Eventually, after a stint as a top-performing salesman within his industry of expertise, AJ decided to follow a new dream, which ironically enough was born in his darkest days watching Coach John do his magic. AJ was not aware a new dream was germinating among all the chaos, but in the back of his head, he was hoping:

"Maybe I can help people like John does someday"

This is a true story based on my business life experiences.

I am AJ the author of this book!

An average person with average talent, ambition and education, can outstrip the most brilliant genius in our society, if that person has clear, focused goals.
                                                    Brian Tracey

The hard lesson I have learned is this – if you don't have the tools to run your own business, or have a tight grip on your Budget, Vision and Sales, the chance of failure is extremely high.

After years of toil along with expensive research , I am finally in a position to use my painful experience to help business owners avoid the cash flow dilemmas as well as other business problems, just like Coach John did.

Except, I have boiled it down to three easy modules to implement: a real live working budget, a systematic sales process, plus a "sticky" vision.

By sticky I mean a boots on the ground plan that everybody understands.

A plan where everyone "sees" how they contribute.

A plan that generates momentum with results.

The coaching / training you will receive are real life experiences, combined with some of the best coaching & training I have paid dearly for, over the last 25 years!

PS: Just for a minute – imagine - if you could wave a magic wand that would change one thing in your business, that is holding you back from where you want to be, what would it be?

As an entrepreneur you probably went into business to be your own boss, to take care of your clients, hoping you would make a little more money than you did working by the hour for someone else.

You probably also were thinking that once you had your business up and running you were going to take a few more vacations, spend a little more time with family and friends and really do the things you always wanted to do. But "somehow" this never happened. Either there wasn't enough money or the timing was never right. If you did squeak out some vacation time, did you come back to a train wreck?, cost more money than you expected?, irate clients etc..?

It doesn't have to be this way. With the help of a business coach you too can turn your business around and have it be all that you had ever hoped!

You may contact the author of this book for more information on how to hire the best coach.

Arne J Raisanen
Strategic Coach & Trainer
Published Author of Don't Miss That Sale
www.arbco.us
arne@arbco.us

HOW IS YOUR BUSINESS?

1) Even the smallest business in the world, needs to know ALL of their cash numbers to survive the ups with the downs in business. What are your numbers?

2) Think about a 10 percent higher closing ratio in your business - What would it mean to you? - What would it look like? You may wonder if it is achievable - I have seen it time and time again.

3) How are you setting your prices? Setting your prices on emotion are the first steps to failure, Setting a live budget will give you the true numbers to set your prices. Never set your prices off what your competitor is charging, they may be wrong too!

4) Finally and perhaps most important, Do you believe your prices? And if you had to raise them 20% - would you?

Arne J Raisanen

KEY POINT:

KEY POINT:

Having a clear vision with a working budget is extremely important to growing a successful business.

KEY POINT:

Measuring and tracking is critical to obtain accurate results in your business.

KEY POINT:

Having a crystal clear understanding of your overhead in your business is vital to your success!

KEY POINT:

Your business plan needs to be crystal clear as to where you're going, how are you going to get there, and what will it look like when you get there.

KEY POINT:

Controlling your business growth will keep you in control of your business. If you're not in control, overhead can overtake your business and spin it out of control!

About the Author

Arne Raisanen, a sales trainer and business coach who has lived in the trenches as a top performing salesman, easily overcame his low price competitors, winning the sale with a much higher sales ticket!

In His book Don't Miss That Sale—Arne teaches why winning at sale number one is so critical to closing the sale.

Arne's business training, together with his coaching, are focused on the three key elements in your business. His real life experiences are taught in each one of his training modules.

(1) Module one - Sales Training
   (Every sales chain has a weak link.. Where is yours?)

(2) Module two - Profit and budget module
   (Running a live bottom up budget)

(3) Module three - Business vision module
   (Creating a culture with a score board for accountability)

Arne Raisanen

arne@arbco.us

Www.arbco.us

The No High Pressure Sales Methodology

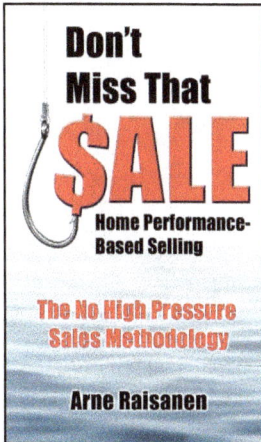

Don't Miss That $ALE
Home Performance-Based Selling

The No High Pressure Sales Methodology

Arne Raisanen

There are two sales to every one sales call. That's regardless of what you're selling, be it products or services.

If your sales call doesn't close, most of the time that means that you didn't close sale number one.

And you can't move to sale number two unless you've first closed sale number one.

What do I mean by two sales? Think of it this way:

Christopher Columbus had to first sell the idea of a voyage to find the Indies, or sale number one, before he could sell the actual voyage to America, or sale number two.

The biggest assumption people in sales make today is that our clients are already sold on the idea that they need to buy this or that product or service. So, we start trying to sell them on reasons to buy from us, before we've sold them on the idea that they really need or want what we have to offer.

This really changes the process of a sales call, doesn't it?

Get your copy today!

http://www.amazon.com/s/ref=nb_sb_noss?url=search-alias%3Daps&field-keywords=Arne+Raisanen

The man who succeeds has a program. He fixes his course and adheres to it. He lays his plans and executes them. He goes straight to his goal. He knows where he wants to go and he knows that he's going to get there. He loves what he's doing and loves the journey that is taking him to the objects of his desires. He is bubbling over with enthusiasm and he is filled with zeal. This is a man who succeeds. – *Anonymous*

For the first time I understand my budget, I can see it work and I can see how an employee pay raise or adding a vehicle changes the company. It is very awesome!

Randy M
Columbia Home Comfort

Arne put us on the path to organize our business. His budgeting system was a real eye opener. We now know where all our money is, and what we need to charge to make a profit, We have a much better understanding on how a budget works.

Steve V
NW HVAC Services Inc.

After working with Arne over the last year, our profits are up 60%. With his knowledge, guidance and enthusiasm he has given us a reason to believe that all of our hard work will pay off and our business will be a success. Thank you again Arne for believing in us!

Scott & April W
RENEWABLE ELECTRIC LLC

www.ingramcontent.com/pod-product-compliance
Lightning Source LLC
Chambersburg PA
CBHW060507220326
41598CB00025B/3586